SWEET INDULGENCES

TQSPEAKS

EXPLICIT NATURE

email: TQSpeaks@yahoo.com
web address :www.Lulu.com/tqspeaks

ISBN 978-0-6151-7148-7

Dedicated to the freak in you.

THANK YOU'S

First and foremost, I thank the Lord for providing me the talent to entertain. My parents, Henry and Joyce Mobley. My sisters, Jade and Dana Mobley love you more than you could ever know. Joanae Mobley. My family The Fosters', Daughtrys', Kennedys', Mayfields' and the Reeds'. My aunt Necie. Uncle Fred. Michael Mayfield that cousin everyone wish they had. Nkenge Mayfield, still my favorite Mayfield. Love you too, Tee. Tanisha I didn't forget you. Billy Harris wish we talked more, miss you. Jackie Carter, one of my closest friends no matter the distance. Kiana Kee, my up north homie that have my back no matter what, a big thank you. Steve Carter you've been like a brother, I appreciate ya. Sharan my sister, love you. Sharanda Houser, I'm still doing my thing. Curtis Houser and John Hill R.I.P. Rashid Hawkins you've always been my brother, from childhood to now, thank you. Mr. Fish for the support. My dog, Sekou Allen for looking out for a brother. Dee, for making us feel comfortable. Abigail, hopefully it will maintain your excitement. Of course the Johnsons', Fred and Monique. Felicia Buck, my big sister who keeps me straight. Tshaka Mitchell my dog for life. Janeen Miller I know you are smiling, you my girl for life. My man, get money partner, Jermaine. Kim Hamilton, a friend no matter the area code. Amar (Amarpep) you always have been so helpful. Anthony Holloway, for the positive words. My barber, Johnny Jackson. Salathiel Chin got to thank you for the push and the support it's very much appreciated. Jonathan "JUVI" Wesley for keeping me focused. Jemeisha Luna your support has been wonderful. My man LAH who tells me I need to be doing more, thank you. Shante Wesley couldn't forget you. Brenda Jackson, thank you for all the nice things you say. Cassandra Eppinger, you are a nut, just take care of my kids. Linda

Glass thanks for checking up on me, I appreciate that. Ms. Detrice, thank you for all your support. (Aunt) C.J. Chavous, just joking. Ms. Hood the sunshine in Life. Kay McLendon you really are not that tough. Laverne Rollins taken over that roll of big sister, they don't know how we roll. Tracey even thought we've never met, we like that. John Andrews, my big homie who looks out all the time. Tony Wilson I know you will enjoy this. Chief Rahim Cromer. Kim Greer you have been there since the beginning thanks. Night time ladies Rhonda, Kendra, Brigette. My weekend ladies at ARC. Antionette Randolph (Caramel Twist) you already know what it is. Beverly Lawrence this should be dedicated to you. Keeli Watson, finally, huh. Andrea Brown my sis from the BK, nothing but love for ya. Monique Ibrahim you are too slick for me. The unforgettable Dawn Brown. For anyone I may have missed, I still appreciate ya.

Prologue:

COCKY

Cocky

I'm not the average Joe
I can write a book on the shit I know ...
And you'll know
You came
When you lose total control of your mind frame
You'll feel drained
See, with me it's not a game
My tongue game
It's insane
It should be locked in a room without a window pane
It's not the same
I'm on a different plane
I give new meaning to "making it rain"
Listen closely as I stimulate your brain
You can put your trust in me
Cause what I'm about to put in you
Is going to leave you good and empty
Attack you with no sympathy
But I'll be real good to the pussy
In fact so good
I could charge a fee
But for you it's free
You'll cum quickly

Constantly and repeatedly
That's what happens when you fuck with a nigga like me
I'll have you throwing your legs up like it's a robbery
Tracing the outside of your legs oh so lightly
Sending chills through your body
Then spreading your legs ever so slightly
Kissing you from the back of your knees
To the lips of your pussy
Tasting your agony
My tongue dancing around your anal cavity
Got you pushing it back into me
At the same time
I got you backing into a corner cowardly
Body trembling visibly
Screaming loudly
"STOP, Don't touch me"
"Put it in." "Just Fuck me."
I know what to do to a woman's body
Yes I'm cocky
Stay rocky
Plus I exercise dick control
So I can handle when the pussy role
But you can't fault me
Cause I eat the pussy properly
Unlike he

You won't be mad at me
I'm real nasty
Not scared to get my face dirty
Whether I take my time and do it slowly
Eating you gradually
Licking all around your wall cavity
Or sucking on your clit hard like a piece of candy
I'll make it come down like it's being pulled by gravity
Is the thought of me all up in your nook and crannies?
Soaking your panties
And if reading this is getting you moist
Wait till I have you cumming to the sound of my voice
I'll be the difference
I'm no apprentice
And if you don't believe me
I can make you a witness
Have you watch me as I part your entrance
Pull back the skin and lick your clitoris
Until you're ready to bust like an appendix
You'll damn near lose consciousness
The tongue is ferocious
Is this the closest?
You ever been
To heaven
To trying to get to that lucky number seven

I'll be your blessing
Your dream
You'll scream
You'll cream
You'll make my face look like it was dipped in a jar of Vaseline
Glistening and dripping
Got your pussy spitting
Ready for a classic dicking
And I'm not talking about Charles
But I'll Suck-Your-Berry till you cum Again
That's when I slide right in
When you can't take the feeling
It's so overwhelming
Creaming so much it looks like
I stuck my dick in a jar of Hellman's

THE SWEETS

RESUMÉ

Good kisser
Ear nibbler
Clit licker
Esophagus tickler
Back bender
Leg opener
Ankle holder
Finger dipper
Ass smacker
Cheek grabber
Pelvis slammer
Headboard banger
Dick layer
Pussy slayer
Leg hiker
Nipple biter
Tittie sucker
And if you have kids
I'll be one hell of a motherfucker
Salad tosser
Shit talker
Nasty like a sewer
Hair puller
Track loosener
Cum producer
Sleep inducer
Sleep aide

Should get paid
Love to get laid
Love the sounds that's made
Soft pecker
Especially around the neck area
Thorough like a food inspector
Multiple orgasms
Cause you should have them
Doggie style
Make you smile
Believe me, I know how
Professional undresser
May take a little time with certain bras
But other than that my skills are up to par
The ability to go far
Eager to please
Won't stop till I satisfy all your needs
Bed shaking
Run to your friend explaining
No longer faking
Type of love making
A magician
Able to make my dick disappear in your incision
No hocus pocus
But you will lose all your focus
Pinky in your derriere
My only fear
You trying to stick something in my rear
Missionary

A visionary
Cause I like the eye contact
But rather be rode from the back
Watching your butt clap
I'm a natural aphrodisiac
Panty wetter
Mood setter
Not a quick nut
A great fuck
Not a big fan of doing it in the butt
But been known to slip up
Can treat you like a slut
Or a queen
I do a little bit of everything
I'm accommodating
I'll be the reason you stop complaining
These are just some of the things that set me above the rest
Not saying I'm the best
But references are available upon request

INDULGENCES

A fat clit
Nice tits
Thick lips
The one below your hips
The type that stick out
Like you're making your lips pout
The fit
How you stroke my dick
I can tell you're really into it
The way you work it
The way you want to quit
When your spot is getting hit
Making you cum
Wait! There goes one
Pure fun
Is that another one?
Unable to calculate the sum
Limping away when we're done
Your facial expression
The connection
The afterward affection
The way your body bends
How you drop down and take it all in

No teeth
Performing like it's your only belief
The noise
How you make me lose my poise
The envy of my boys
Open to toys
No ploys
Yet you're so unaware
Of how much you really care
I'm constantly catching you when you stare
The way you crave my touch
Want me just as much
How it gets so wet
Make me sweat
The side bets
About what we're going to do to each other
I'll be the sucker
You'll be the suckee
Cause I love eating pussy
The taste
Putting it on my face
Especially when it's shaved
Watch how my tongue misbehave
A memory you'll save
That look

That way your body shook
The sound of skin slapping
The passion
The reaction
You never ration
IT'S MINE
Reads the caption
You just do me right
It's so tight
It's my kryptonite
Making me explode like dynamite
So why fight
When your sex is contagious
Outrageous
The sweetest indulgence
Love it in abundance
It's my only weakness
That's is why I'm constantly walking around here
With a hard penis

PEKING

This is just an introduction
To the way my mouth function
Letting you know it's all about the suction
And the production
Of you cumming
I'll have you thinking I'm the devil
How I take your body to another level
Looking for Bellevue
Just needing someone to talk to
Like wow "He's special"
Flirting with your opening
Driving you crazy with the sound of my slurping
See, I know you were hoping
Didn't believe the words that were spoken
Now you're like that shit is "Mind Blowing"
And yet, you don't even know what it is
Maybe it's the aggressiveness
The way I attack the middle of your pelvis
Helpless
Screaming like you just seen Elvis
But whatever it is
You like what I do to your clitoris
Even the way I lick your anus
I'll make you famous
The pressure is continuous
Even to the finish
While the pleasure is endless

I'll have you speechless
Pussy leaking
Clit peeking
I'll be all that you're seeking
It's the reason
I'm known as the PEKing
It's the manner in which I be speaking
I'm fluent
I'll have you translucent
It's just the way that I do it
A little different
Very persistent
Results are evident
So I understand why you're a little hesitant
Scared you just might like it
Or you might get addicted
Just from the way I lick it
I'll have your pussy thinking I'm scared of commitment
The way my tongue split it
Leaving you discombobulated
Loving the way I just ate it
I talk it
While my tongue walk it
The way I gnaw
Got you where you can't take it anymore
Ready to claw
Your way through the door
Like you're a character in the movie "SAW"
Slow licking

Tongue sticking
Legs shivering
Cum trickling
Eyes popping
Oh Godding!
Damn near crying
Oozing like tree sap
Clit so fat
It overlaps
Sucking on your flaps
Biting down and pulling back
Making your stomach muscles contract
You won't know how to react
Face contorted like you been hit with the plague
Watching you beg
Locking your legs
So you can't run
Worried about what my tongue just done
As you cum
Repeatedly
Looking at me
Like it's the first time seeing me
Satisfied completely
And, yes I'm cocky
But you just love what I do to your body
Regretting nothing
Remembering all the times I had you cumming

PEKing = Pussy Eating King

9

CAN I HAVE A TASTE

I just want to lay you on your stomach
You have the type of ass that most women covet
Ass abundant
Make any man want to plummet
To the depths of your soul
Learning every mole
Exploring all your folds
With forefingers and thumbs
Tracing the alphabet with my tongue
Got you ready to cum
With so many ways to eat you
On your back spread eagle
On my knees eager to please you
A feeding frenzy
Sucking you till you're good and empty
Satisfying a hunger
Slowing it down so it last longer
So the climax is that much stronger
You'll think something's wrong
Cause I've been down there so long
I'll have you so gone
You'll be using my ears to hold on
Wanting everything I have to give
The way I suck your ovaries like olives
That will have you hit different octaves
See, my tongue is trained

To flicker like a flame
That will have you calling the Lord's name in vain
Without any shame
Losing your composure
As my tongue slide back and forth
Between your vulva
Bringing you closer
To your apex
Making your muscles contract and flex
Call it my mouth casting a hex
Or granting wishes
The French kisses on your clitoris
Is pure stimulus
Leaving me drenched in your wetness
Lifting your garage
So I can give your clit a tongue massage
That will have it enlarged
Fully erected
The bed soaking wet
Your hair's a wreck
From the beads of sweat
And I know how much you hate getting your hair wet
So I'll pay for your next wash n set
Anytime anyplace
Just put it on my face
I like the way you roll your waist
Using the headboard to control the pace
Holding your ass in place

Cause you like to run when you cum
So now I won't have to chase
When that expression appears on your face
And your love starts to ooze from your space
With a worn look like you just won a race
You'll be glad you gave me a taste

IN THE KITCHEN

In the kitchen
Where the object is digesting
I'm start with a little light munching
Bringing your breast together like a family function
Applying the right amount of suction
Causing your nipples to stand at attention
To show you the spontaneity isn't missing
Performing like two skilled mathematicians
I add my digits as your legs practice it's division
Giving me room to play in your incision
That'll have you dripping
My fingers glistening
Almost feels like you're ready for entering
Tasting your nectar
So enamored by the flavor
I drop to my knees like you're my savior
As my tongue dances in between your labia
Taking you further
With your leg draped over my shoulder
Stopping as you get closer
So we can continue by the sofa
With me bending you over
It's no surprise
How fast my nature rise
As I position myself between your thighs
Hearing those soft cries
As I penetrate

Your pussy percolates
As my magic stick makes your ass levitate
Humping and pumping
At a steady rate
Trying real hard to concentrate
The feeling is so great
It feels like I'm about to detonate
Your body begins to shake
The sounds you make
Hissing like a snake
The juices the friction creates
Got me losing focus
Especially the way you stick out your ass
Like here "poke this"
So I take a 5 second intermission
Change positions
My vision
You riding me from the opposite direction
Sliding up and down on my erection
The way your pussy heat
Engulfs my meat
Vaporizing the pre-cum I secrete
Paralyzing me from my head to my feet
So weak
Barely able to speak
The way you hop
Pop
And rock
Your hot box

On my cock
Hitting your spot
That got you on a feverous attack
As you look back
The look in my eyes
Says my nature is about to meet it's demise
Ready to erupt
Movements become abrupt
The way you're backing it up
Got my dick bout to throw up
But I try to refrain
And it's hard
Cause the feeling is insane
Got me calling your name
Grabbing your mane
You shudder because you just came
Wanting me to do the same
While it drains
Down the side of my leg
You beg
For me to let it go
As your juices continue to flow
Your sugar walls
Absorb
My explosion
Setting off multiple implosions
Creating a whole lot of commotion
From the circular motion
Leaving me frozen

With my mouth hanging open
Your body jerking
Breaking down the dam to your ocean
Drowning in your devotion
Flaccid
And damn near whipped
The way you just sank my battleship

CONTROL

Overwhelm by the sexiness you display
And since I don't really know what to say
I'm just walk up to you and turn you around
Moving you hair out the way
Fingers caressing your neckline
Taking my time
Kissing you along your spine
Slowing down as I approach your waistline
Drop to my knees to worship your shrine
Dividing your center line
As I dine between your behind
Drinking you like fine wine
Giving you a feeling that so sublime
You'll start to grind
Pushing me back so I'm lying supine
You must have read my mind
How you start choking my chicken
While holding your butt open
Your clit showing
My tongue circling
Your clit swollen
Got my mojo working
But you break my concentration
With deep mouth penetration
My penis tickles your esophagus
At the same time my tongue teases your clitoris
Got your juices flowing continuous

Loving how I place my tongue between your cheeks like a thong
But it's the taste of my shlong
That has you so turned on
Have you be ready to jump on
Slide on
Ride along
To the rhythm of your own song
Hopping off my face and easing down
Grabbing my ankles as you start to pound
Skin slapping isn't the only sound
Got you acting like a clown
Permanent smile
But I'm astound
When you hop off
Telling me you want to use your mouth to get me off
Plus you're trying to see what you taste like on me
Your movement fast and steady
Like a woodpecker to a tree
Letting me know it's all about me
With a look in your eye
That says you're about to suck me dry
All I have to say
"You're welcome to try"
Leaned back
Head back
Eyes closed up on elbows
While you curl them toes
Enough power to suck a golf ball through a garden hose
The type of suction

That leads to a premature eruption
I see you're a master at your craft
Licking me up and down my shaft
Around the tip
Making popping sounds with your lips
Engulfing my dick using spit
Oh shit!
You got me climbing walls
Sucking balls and all
I can tell this what you prefer if given a choice
The way your pussy getting moist
Oh! You're into it
The movement the way you make love to it
Don't know if it's your stroke
Just seems like you knows what works
But you don't treat it like a job
The way you bob
Your hands motions like you're turning a knob
The right amount of slob
My God
You got me ready to succumb
My body feeling numb
I'm about to c-c-c-c-c-cum
Damn I just came
Your new name
Jaws of Life
Got to thank my kids for their sacrifice
For they so dearly paid the price
When every last one of them got swallowed

Leaving me hallow
Limp
While you're just staring at me as you wipe your lip

IMAGINATION

You just don't know what I'm going through
How bad I want you
Just watching you
The way you sashay
So much I could say
You're like, every man's dream
Can't help but to think about ways to make your body scream
Just sit back and listen while I paint the scene
Show you what I really mean
See, I got this thing I do with my tongue
While applying pressure I have a song I hum
It's called "getting you sprung"
It'll make you explode like a gun
Better yet
A cannon
Can you imagine?
Total satisfaction
Non-stop action
You're body will feel like it's been put in traction
I'll be all over you
Making you feel like you're being tag team
You'll have to use the pillow to stifle your scream
When I dive between
Licking you clean
Like a dog and his favorite cuisine
I'll turn you into a fiend
Head spinning like a cogwheel in a machine

Reenacting that Exorcist scene
Your body will cream
Repeatedly
While your legs shake violently
You're eyes will roll into the back of your head
Resembling the un-dead
I'll make dips
And take sips with the use of fingertips
That'll put a quiver in your lips
That'll make you want to do flips
As I guide my ship
Between your hips
Before dropping my anchor
I'll tease you with just the tip
Work between your slits
Erecting your clit
Leave you so spent
You'll feel like you came and went
In and out of consciousness
Breathless
My sex is so infectious
You'll be giving it up
Like this was a stickup
Getting all up in your guts
You'll feel like you just did 1000 sit-ups
Giving your entire body the hiccups
Sore, but you'll still want more
From position to position
The bedroom to countertop in the kitchen

My mission
To maintain a constant pelvic to pelvic collision
Bending you like hinges
With smooth repetitions
Hitting that spot that releases your tension
Producing a milky white secretion
That can cause labored breathing
While sweat profusely seeping
So deny me
There's no reason
And you can't lie
What you're hearing is pleasing
So stop turning your head to the side
Trying to hide you eyes
Because you know they'll reveal all you try to hide
As your vagina walls start to collide
Your legs can't help but divide
You'll be begging me to touch you on the inside
Pulling your panties aside
Licking you from your front to your backside
Giving you a feeling you can't hide
You'll try to take it in stride
As I slide my pride inside
The body never lied
Once we coincide
You'll swear your soul just cried
By the time I'm finished
All your doubts will have died

QUICKIE

From the moment I close the door
I'll have clothes hitting the floor
It'll be a crime to waste time
Staring at your behind
You know exactly what's on my mind
Locking lips
Our saliva mix
Hands on tits
The squeezing and caressing
Gives you fits
Got you gyrating your hips
Wanting me to scratch that itch
Zipping down my pants
Reaching in my open slit
Grabbing my dick
Stroking it
Rubbing your thumb over the tip
Putting my hands in your shorts
Playing with your clit
I can feel your wetness starting to drip
You tighten your grip
Not one
But two fingers slip
Between your lips
Quick
Upward movements

Pulling my hand out drenched in your fluid
Ready to do it
Back peddling
My oral presentation is the type that's bed wetting
I can see why
That thought is a little unsettling
Being led
To the bed
Without a word being said
You commence to giving me head
The type to make a brother beg
Kissing and licking all around the head
A specialist
Who method is effective
Moving your head up and down
So fast it could be considered reckless
Movement effortless
A couple of minutes a few seconds
My semen is contagious
How you catch it in your mouth
Using your legs as earmuffs
I'm about to go south
Returning the favor
Sucking the area between your labia
See, now your clits in danger
Using my tongue like a skilled wrangler
I'll have you whipped
Taking hits to your clit
Like a boxer to a speed bag

You'll be looking for something to grab
As I slowly drag
My tongue between your buttocks
You're going to need detox
I'll have you hooked on a different type of rocks
The kind that's called getting yours off
The thought of me
Will have you ready to take your clothes off
Thinking about getting your pussy ate
And your salad tossed
Don't forget the dick of course
Which is pointing north
Far from stoic
When the pussy lowered
Sliding down my pole
Watching your hips roll
Like a spoon in a mixing bowl
It's laced in gold
So I'm trying to exercise dick control
I see that feeling has taken hold
Cause your looking for something to hold
As your orgasm fall from your folds
Raising up off my meat
Your pussy leaks
Legs weak
As you stagger to your feet
Only to fall back in your seat
With a look that says
We need to do this at least twice a week

PREREQUISITE

I know it's a woman's prerequisite
Before you stick
Your dick
You must lick
The clit
Pay dividends
To gain entrance
So I abide
With pride
Many men have cried
Because that hide can't be denied
And that profile of you lying on your side
Let's just say my actions are justified
Pulling your thong to the side
As I slide
My head between your thighs
A welcome surprise
As my tongue guides
Along the walls of your insides
Your body complies
I can tell from the sounds
I'm making more than just your thong come down
Flipping that leg around
And I'm back on your mound
Like a pitcher ready to deliver
With your knees perpendicular
My vernacular

Will have you throwing your head back
Like a pez dispenser
With your eyes closed
Breathing through your mouth and not your nose
As the feeling grows
Intensifies
You don't even realize
You start rotating your hips counter-clockwise
Ready to spill your insides
Amazed how I'm keeping up with you
Have you thinking my head is attached to a swivel
Preparing you for my penis
From your gluteus to your clitoris
Call me Mr. Cunnilingus
Wondering if I am a thespian
Impersonating a lesbian
Claiming my technique is pure perfection
How I hold your clit
Between my lips
With quick flicks
Of my tongue
Strum like a thumb
On a guitar string
Making your body sing
Cream
Flow like a stream
Your body leans
And rocks wit' it
Inducing Rapid Eye Movement

But I'm not done
The object is to make you cum
And this is just round one
I'll know when you really lost it
Cause it'll pour out like a faucet
But I'm in no rush
Up and down
Long even strokes like a painter's brush
That'll make you gush
Knowing if I drink too much you'll call me a lush
Still I increase the speed
Giving you the relief you need
It'll feel like you just peed
As my tongue goes to work
Like I'm eating my favorite dessert
The howl
And the way your body jerks
Acts as an alert
Preparing me as I get soaked
Like a pregnant woman's water just broke
Damn near choke
When you start to squirt
A small lake
Harlem shake
Like New York just got hit by a earthquake
Round two
You're just about through
By the time I complete my obligations
You'll be begging for penetration

BACK SHOTS

On bended knee
At the a right degree
I enter slowly
Giving you all of me
Placing one hand above your booty
The other hand full of hair for stability
You start giving it back to me
Bucking wildly
Bellowing your plea
"Give us free"
While trying to flee
But, I got you in my bracket
Making a whole lot of racket
Especially when I slap it
You know you like that shit
When I reach around
And finger your clit
The movement
So fluent
Every time you back into it
Howling like the wind in the breeze
On hands and knees
Putting an arch in your back like parenthesis
Handling you with ease
Making me promising to never leave
The back shots are so proper
It'll have you calling my momma

Thanking her
Cause I'm shaped like a comma
And you know how it curves to the left
So, when I swerve it's the stroke of death
Hitting that nerve that releases your stress
I'm here to serve and give you my best
I'm a virtuoso
So
Even if you have your period
I have ways we can work around it
Not trying to make you sick
But I'm bout it bout it
I'll either stick it
Or lick it
And before you say forget it
Think about it
See, I know exactly where your clit sit
I'll just spread your lips
So, I could lick your clit
Till your pussy spit
Without getting blood on the tip....
But...hey that's another topic
What you figure?
I'm a nasty nigga
I don't know if it's the position
Or the vision
Of my dick going in and out of your incision
The sounds of bodies slapping
How your neck be snapping

I just love pushing against your cushion
How the suction
Have me on the verge of nutting
Lost of bodily functions
Yet steady pumping
Punctuating
Head board banging
Making my point to bring you to exclamation
Watching your bosom
Knock back and forth like a pendulum
Thinking about how good it would feel to slide my dick in between them
Pounding you like a drum
Watching the white secretions build on my dick
As you cum
Lying there numb
Nothing but silence
From what I just done
Till I hear the sound of gas
Oh!
That's just your pussy impersonating
Your ass

INTIMATE CONTACT

I like the way we interact
Our body contact
The way you react
When I kiss the small of your back
That sound you make from getting your ass smacked
The way you make your butt clap
When I put my tongue in your butt crack
Pushing hairs back so I can lick that
I see how unprepared you are as my mouth makes impact
The way you throw your head back
Feels like your clit is being attacked
Rapid tongue brushing
That'll have your geyser gushing
My tongue navigation produces sweet sensations
As I lick all your favorite places
Turning you into anything but gracious
The way you humping and pumping my face
Increasing the pace
Gyrating
Legs shaking
And that's just from my oral stimulation
Faster than the board of education
In one night
Taking you from first grade to graduation
Since the beginning of creation
Like Adam and his apple contemplation

I'll be your greatest temptation
More than just infatuation
It's mental anticipation
Succumbing to your every temptation
No more hesitation
Your hearts racing
You want penetration
The kind that cause hyperventilation
"GASP"
"GASP"
As I insert my shaft
Taking your knees over my shoulder
To turning you over
Pulling you closer
Pulling your hair
To whispering in your ear
Do you want it right here
While you're screaming
YEAH!
YEAH!
"Right there"
"Don't stop I'm almost there"
You'll shed a tear
As I enter from the rear
Causing epileptic like convulsions
Your body shaking uncontrollable with each explosion
Your heart just been stolen
Overflowing with emotion

As I ride every wave of your ocean
Leaving me drenched in your love potion
Steady injections
Taking all suggestions
"Faster"
"Slower"
As I gliding in and out of tight sections
Throbbing and flexing
Until you receive my full blessing
Session after session
It's more than just a physical connection
It's pure heaven
The only way to describe the pleasure
When our bodies cum together

COPULATE

It's how we relate
In more ways than one can calculate
Like the way we communicate
With that look in your eye
That says you just can't wait
You don't even hesitate
Your legs just separate
Making my mouth salivate
Cause I know you like to be ate
Filling my plate
With your protein shake
Calling yourself increasing my intake
Which I appreciate
But you and I both know
It's just a better way to irrigate
Making it easier to enter Heaven's gates
So I concentrate where life originates
Using my fingers to facilitate
The figure-eights my tongue makes
Doing whatever it takes
Even if my tongue aches
Clit going to stimulate
Hips gyrate while back elevates
Waistlines rotate heart rates escalate
Body shakes causing sound to escape
Causing my limbs to elongate

Begging to participate
Plans to penetrate
Our movements coordinate
Till lips pulsate and juices emanate
Performing to a stalemate
Recuperate
Then duplicate
You're my soul mate
I knew from the first date
It had to be fate
And all the ones before you
Were just mistakes

PLEASHER

There is nothing better
Than giving a woman pleasure
That's why I take extreme measures
Taking of your clothes
While nibbling at your earlobe
Then letting my tongue probe
Down to the nape of your neck
Tending to the areas of neglect
Taking a slow trek
To produce a lasting effect
Going lower, slower, showing love to your shoulders
Before engulfing your entire areola
Leaving your nipples standing at attention
Sucking all your fingers
Careful not to linger
Cause I can see your body getting eager
Biting your bottom lip
As my tongue dips past your hips
Looking you in your eye
Planting kisses on your inner thighs
While you let out a soft cry
Taking my time
Licking you from front to behind
My mission is to please
I'll even kiss the back of your knees
Turning up the degrees

While bending you at the knees
Propping you up on your elbows
Sucking your toes
Making my way to your asshole
Just let your inhibitions go
Lean back and enjoy the show
Yeah, I know
It sounds a little heinous
Talking about licking your anus
But once I spread your butt cheeks
And your ass and my tongue meet
I guarantee it'll curl your feet
You'll be pulling up the bed sheet
Screaming in exuberance
As I encircle the circumference
Using my face to create a clearance
Teasing the entrance
While my nose rub up against
Your exposed clitoris
Your body will experience the difference
Of a tongue penetrating every entrance
Pulling out all the resources
That causes rigor mortis
With timely added pauses
That will have you begging me to continue
Serving you like you're something on the menu
So don't think it's something you have to do
Or earn

Cause we don't have to take turns
Your pleasure is my only concern
You can use my face as a churn
I'd love to see you squirm
As my tongue wiggle like a worm
Making you cream like butter
And your eyelids flutter
While the words you try to utter
Come out as a st- st- st- stutter

A Lovers Fight

ROUND 1

I have a tongue display
That'll turn your body into chocolate soufflé
It's not what you say
It's how you say it
I just let my tongue explain it
Listen carefully because it gets deep
Leaving you feeling whipped and beat
Showing you how I eat
With my hands
Making demands
"Hold this leg"
"Let me hear you beg"
"Open up wider"
As I slowly devour
Using my hands as a divider
As the saliva helps my tongue become a smoother glider
Setting you on fire
The way I roll my tongue like a tire
Up and down
And all around
Slowly breaking you down
Carnivorous how I attack your clitoris
The stimulus is intuitive
Your wetness is generous
And we're not even finished
Continuing to dazzle you with my English
My tongue should be considered a genius

An I.Q.
That can make you
Cum repeatedly
Excuse me, I mean Cum Laude
Turning your body
Into a cumming out party
Hearing you scream
Watching you crème
Melt like ice cream
The theme
Vanilla
My favorite flavor
You know that stuff that flows from between you labia
Taking you up like an escalator
More like an elevator
Hoister
Have you plastered up against the wall like a poster
Sitting on my shoulders
Introducing my mouth to your vulva
Like a explorer learning a new culture
Continually going over
To I'm familiar with your interior
It's not going too take long
Because my technique is superior
All up in between your cavities
With the energy to outlast a drawer full of batteries
Once my tongue break through
You're through
The damage it'll do

Loitering in your vestibule
Nibbling on your clit like a child does vegetables
Digesting you
Have the neighbors think I'm killing you
Like what's going over there
Have you sounding like a wounded bear
As I emptying your vault
A feeling that can't be fought
A feeling you sought
A skill you wish everyone was taught
See, I know what you want
Laying you face down
Staring at that pretty brown round
Grabbing you by the wrist
Holding your hands outward bound
Using the leverage as I start to pound
Knees bent
Short quick powerful movements
Got your head snapping to it
Hit after hit
Delivering fulfillment and punishment
Got you on the ropes about to lose it
As you start gushing fluid
No choice but to let it go
First round TKO

2nd ROUND KNOCKOUT

You're ready for round 2?
Thought you were through
What you going to do?
After I just put it on you
I had your body humming and cumming
At least that's what I thought
She just looked at me and didn't say nothing
Out of breath
Nothing left
A feeling I see she's trying to compress
With her palms on my chest
A hunch in her shoulders
That's says this is not over
Franticly
Throwing it at me
Repeatedly whispering to me
"Give it to me"
"Let it go"
"That's it daddy"
Mounting her attack
Pushing me back
While putting an arch in her back
Damn! The way she makes her walls contract
The way her body snaps
Raise up
Come down with impact
Making a thunderous smack

Repeatedly
Like when hands clap
Have a brother not knowing how to act
Or react
When she slides back
Without losing contact
Holding my head in the entrance of her gap
Rotating around the tip
Rolling her hips
Taking dips
Giving me fits
Trying not to quit
But I'm on the verge of losing it
She slides off
And put her lips to it
Engulfing my dick
Like a phagocyte
Hers jaws so tight
Trying to fight
A left, a right
She sees it in my eyes
It's not my night
Trying not to cum too soon
But it's like a vacuum
I know I've met my doom
Starting to shake
It's too late
As she start milking my dick as I ejaculate
Using my dick like it was a straw in a vanilla milk shake

ROUND 3

So you made me cum but I'm not done
Nor am I Moses but I'll part you like the Red Sea
Throw your legs up in a V
Eat you like I am hungry
The way I go to the body
I'll have your legs wobbly
It's a guarantee
Far from luck
How I make your body buck
Pussy up-chuck
From getting your clit sucked and plucked
Tongue fucked and your butt stuck
Without taking a breath
Face first
Like a pie eating contest
Starting in the middle
Playing your clit like a fiddle
Working my way around your edges
Glad you trimmed your hedges
Cause in one swift motion
I'll have you wide open
Slurping
Got your clit growing
Swollen
About to lose your bodily functions
With the right amount of suction
In conjunction

With finger fucking
The quick flicker
Watching as your clit gets bigger
Your lip quiver biting on it like it's dinner
From the pleasure I deliver
Painting the perfect picture
An instant classic
Call me Mr. Fantastic
Moving my tongue like it's made of elastic
How it contorts
To your vaginal walls
As you do your best impression of Niagara Falls
Even got you butt giving applause
Without taking a pause
Spreading your butt cheeks
It's nothing I won't eat
Giving your ass a real treat
That'll have your ass and pussy trying to compete
But I'll make your butt the envy
After you see what I do with my pinky
Sliding it in ever so gently
While I eat you intently
Mouth smacking
Body unraveling
It's that reaction
That extends my erection
Call it a second wind
That allows me to slide right back in
Immediately and forcefully

Moving rapidly
The orgasm is almost instantaneously
Mind in a frenzy
Leaking profusely
"Damn you're so wet"
With you legs behind my neck
Grabbing the mattress
As I bang your pelvis
No where to run
Just helpless
Coming down hard
Got you calling for the Lord
Screaming
"Harder"
"Harder"
" Just like that"
"Fuck me"
That's when I stop momentarily
Watching you go crazy
Begging me
"Please don't stop"
Trying to slide up my cock
Got you ready to pop
So I continue
Bringing your legs down for a better view
Watching as I slide in and out of you
As your clit runs along that big vein
Unable to count the number of times you just came
With your body drained

You have no shame in lying in the wet stain
Armed with just a smile
I got you ready to throw in the towel

The
Controversy

Making Love vs Fucking

MAKING LOVE

I know how to express my love for you
Know how to follow through
From your hair follicle
To the bottom of your feet
Give your whole body a treat
I'll make it sensual
Light candles
Spread rose petals
Have the bed looking like a kid with freckles
Take you to the next level
Show you what should be acceptable
While I'm making love to you
Other dudes just try to catch wreck
I start with small pecks
From your lips to your cheek
To your neck
Ambiance starts to take effect
I can smell your panties getting wet
Kissing caressing
Slowly undressing
Rubbing touching
The opposite of fucking
Everything real intimate
I get into it
Can't help it I'm passionate
My tongue and stick is magic
Our movement

Will be rhythmic
Like we're doing it to music
And although it's playing in the background
It's also used to drown out the sound
Of you howling like a hound
When I drop down
Face to face with your clit
Quickly grabbing it between my lips
Got you taking breaths in short sips
Far from coy
Between your legs giving you pure joy
Like a boy and his favorite toy
The type of foreplay
That the after effect will last all day
Have your mind spinning like I'm molding clay
Making your body sway
Like a leaf on a windy day
Moving your limbs this way
That way
Out my way
Applying constant pressure so the feeling stays
Frozen you lay
Mouth open
Like a mannequin on display
As my tongue conveys
A message
That allows for easy passage
Shoulders slumped
Slow calculated pumps

Adding a little thump
Until your body erupt
Stroking your hair
Whispering in your ear
I'll be giving you the good wood
For as long as I could
Doing all that I can
Not trying to be the man
Saying, "I'll do you all night"
See I'm going to take my time
And do you right
It's about quality
Not quantity
Unless you're talking about
The number of times you'll be cumming for me
It's no real controversy
Some dudes just don't know how to treat pussy

FUCKING

Well, I'm that dude that's just nasty
I'm not trying to be all fancy
Touchy feely
I'm just trying to smash some pussy
Some dudes put the pussy up on a pedal stool
I just make it drool
Ladies don't worry because you'll have a ball
You might even fall
I'm that dude that'll hit you in a bathroom stall
The parking lot at the mall
Have you making late night booty calls
I'll fuck you to you're spoiled
Licking, sticking
I do it all
Treat the pussy?
I beat it up
We can fuck
In the back of the truck
Legs up
On headrest
Half dress
Pumping till we're out of breath
Biting your breast
Through your shirt
Making your body jerk
Falling back from all the energy you exert
Trying to get it together so we can make it back to work

Shit, even at work you could get it

In a closet

Sucking your tits

Fingering your clit

Got you reaching for my dick

You squat and sit

Using a glob of spit

To line my dick

Your head begin to bob

As you slob my knob

Have me reaching for the doorknob

For leverage

The way you take it in

Looks like my head been severed

Strokes are slow and measured

Slurping

While co-workers on the other side of the door lurking

Or in the office

Filling all your orifices

Praying it don't result in any job loses

Taking mental pauses

You won't be able to get me off your mind

I'll have you saying anyplace anytime

Sticking it out, so I can hit it from behind

Over a balcony

For everyone to see

At a movie

I could do you

You could do me

Stadium seating
Conducive for eating
How they rock back
Matter of fact
Just sit on my lap
And let me tap that from the back
I'm the type that'll flirt then lift your skirt
Move your thong to the side
As we ride
The elevator
As my dick slide back and forth
Between your labia
Pressing buttons
Unbutton buttons
Just straight fucking
No fear
Anywhere
Pulling hair
Smacking your rear
Back-shots
You on top
You on your belly
Missionary
Getting sweaty
Till you quit
Talking shit
Pulling muscles
Got your hair looking like you been in a tussle
Bent over the sofa

Legs over shoulders
Banging you into a coma
Budussy is the aroma
You just might love me when it's all over

TQSPEAKS IS THE AUTHOR OF WHAT'S YOUR SCENARIO. HE'S BROOKLYN BRED NOW RESIDING IN ATLANTA WITH HIS FAMILY.